The Fine Art of Reading

The Fine Art
of Reading

by

David Cecil

SOUVENIR PRESS

First published in 1949 as *Reading as One of the Fine Arts*, by the Clarendon Press, Oxford

Published in 1957 as part of the *The Fine Art of Reading and Other Literary Studies* by Constable and Company Limited, London

This Edition published 2001 by Souvenir Press Ltd., 43 Great Russell Street, London WC1B 3PA

ISBN 0 285 63600 6

Typeset by Photoprint, Torquay, Devon

Printed and bound in Italy

To
Cynthia Asquith

'You common people of the skies
What are you when the moon shall rise!'

'For the earthly beauty is a shadow and image of the heavenly beauty.'

The Fine Art
of Reading

AFTER HIS DEATH, said the poet Yeats, he
would like to assume

. . . such a form as Grecian goldsmiths make
Of hammered gold and gold enamelling
To keep a drowsy Emperor awake;
Or set upon a golden bough to sing
To lords and ladies of Byzantium
Of what is past, or passing, or to come.

But in fact, he applied the same process to
his thoughts whenever he made them into a
poem. So do all other creative writers. Are
they not—like the goldsmiths—practicians of
a fine art?

Alas, this is too often forgotten when literature is made a subject of academic study. The academic approach and method was devised for other subjects: for philosophy, for mathematics, for history; intellectual, ascetic studies, concerned with facts and ideas and whose aim is the discovery of impersonal, objective truth. When they turn their attention to the fine arts, academic persons tend to treat them in the same way. With literature this is easy. For literature is not a pure art like music. It also deals with facts and ideas and can be studied with a view to discovering objective truth. It is possible, for instance, to examine Pope's works as an example of eighteenth-century use of English; or *Paradise Lost* as a manual of theology; or to read *Jane Eyre* in order to find out how governesses lived in the reign of Queen Victoria. Possible, but mistaken! For one thing, these books are not safe guides for the purpose. Pope—just because he was a genius—is a less typical exponent of eighteenth-century English than are the Dunces whom he satirized: Milton's theology, to judge by the controversy that still rages about it, is somewhat confused: and very few Victorian governesses, one is relieved to learn, led a life like Jane Eyre's. Moreover, to read these books for information is not to read them with the purpose that their authors intended. Art is not like mathematics or philosophy. It is a subjective, sensual, and highly personal activity in which facts and ideas are the servants of fancy and feeling; and the artist's first aim is not truth but delight. Even when, like Spenser, he wishes to instruct, he seeks to do so by delighting. It follows that the primary object of a student of literature is to be delighted. His duty is to enjoy himself: his efforts should be directed to developing his faculty of appreciation. For this reason, I have thought it worth while considering what exactly the development of such a faculty entails.

I hesitated for some time before deciding to do this, because so much of what I had to say had already been said by greater men than myself; and especially by Walter Pater. Pater

is a neglected author to-day. One can understand why. His mind is a little languid, his
style a little mannered, and himself a little
over-serious. There is something ludicrous in
expounding the art of enjoyment in so hu-
shed and solemn a tone. All the same, it is a
great pity to neglect Pater. To a degree un-
paralleled among English writers, he com-
bined the two qualities essential for critical
appreciation—common sense and uncommon sensibility. So that not only could he
respond intensely to the most diverse kinds
of art, but he had the shrewdness to analyse
his responses, and argue from them to arrive
at a general view of the scope and nature of
appreciation. As never before he made its first
principles clear: he laid foundations on which
anyone who works in the same field should
build. I like to think that I have a spiritual
predecessor at Oxford in Pater, unworthy to
follow him though I may be; and to fancy that
his shade, with its pensive glance and ghostly
grey moustache, has left its sequestered

haunt in his panelled rooms at Brasenose to hover benignly near me.

I was further discouraged from discoursing on appreciation by the fact that what had not been said already about the matter by Pater and others seemed, most of it, too obvious to be worth saying at all. This, however, is not so, to judge by the number of so-called experts on the subject who appear to be ignorant of it. How many professional critics continue all their lives complacently content with a taste narrow, faddy and inconsistent; while some academic teachers seem to take a perverse pride in possessing a taste so queasy as hardly to be able to stomach any books at all. Indeed, to enjoy literature as it should be enjoyed is a task of immense difficulty; requiring, in addition to common sense and uncommon sensibility, faith, hope, charity, humility, patience and most of the other Christian virtues. It also involves a long and unhurried process of self-training. To begin with we must learn to start from the right place, to get the right line of approach. This means understanding what it is that we are approaching. We must have a right notion of the nature of a work of art, and, more particularly, must we realize that it is the result of two impulses. First of all, it is the record of a personal vision. Some aspect of the artist's experience strikes him with such freshness and intensity that he feels impelled to communicate it to other people. Gray wants to write down what he felt and thought when he took a stroll in Stoke Poges churchyard one twilit evening in 1742. This, however, was not his only motive in writing his poem. People do not become painters simply because they want to paint some particular object. They do it because they like painting; because the creative instinct in them finds fulfilment in constructing a pleasing pattern in line and colour. It is the same with writers. If Gray had only wanted to put down the facts about his feelings in the churchyard, he could have done it with less trouble in prose. But he also liked writing verses. The creative writer is always partly inspired by his desire to construct a pleasing object in his chosen medium. Yeats, in the passage I have quoted, wants to sing of 'what is past, or passing, or to come', but he also wishes to do it in a form made of 'hammered gold and gold enamelling'. This double impulse—to express the individual vision and to work in a particular medium—actuates every true artist. It is the union of the two that produces the phenomenon that we call a work of art.

A unique phenomenon: the result of an unprecedented and unrepeatable fusion of subject and personality and form. It is just this uniqueness which is the object of our appreciation. For in it resides its vital virtue, its aesthetic quality; only so far as it possesses it, does it exist as a work of art at all. And our task is to discern this quality and respond to it. If we feel so disposed, we can go on to try to analyse it into its component elements. Then we turn from readers into critics. But if we have not first perceived it accurately, we shall not be able to criticize it justly. Our first aim must be to see the work as it is.

This means accepting the limitations by which its individuality is defined. There is the limitation of the personal vision. I have said that the artist is inspired by his experience; but no artist, not even Shakespeare or Tolstoy, is so receptive as to be inspired by all his experience Only certain things will strike deep enough into the fundamental stratum of his personality to fertilize his genius: only to a certain amount of what he sees and hears will he respond strongly enough for his record of it to be coloured and energized by his individual vitality. As a consequence, it is only in so far as his work deals with these aspects of his experience that it has aesthetic life. Every writer has, inevitably, a limited creative range. The reader should always be on the look-out to note the scope of this range. Nor should he blame the writer for remaining within it. On the contrary, he should realize that only in so far as he does so is he a successful artist. It was foolish of Charlotte Brontë to condemn Jane Austen for not depicting the full fury of the passions. It would have been equally foolish if Jane Austen had criticized Charlotte Brontë for a morbid pre-occupation with personal emotion. Charlotte Brontë was not a cool and healthy-minded person; and the spectacle of the passions in violent action did not kindle Jane Austen's creative spark. It is no use blaming a writer for failing to do something he never intended to do; and, most likely, would not have made a success of if he had.

Equally must the reader accept the limitations imposed by form. There are critics who have condemned Ben Jonson's comedies because they lack the delicate sentiment and lyrical grace they find so agreeable in Shakespeare's; and who have argued from this that Ben Jonson was a coarse and prosaic person. In fact he was nothing of the kind, as anybody can discover by reading *The Sad Shepherd*. But the satirical type of comedy which Ben Jonson chose to write could not admit sentiment and lyrical grace without destroying that unity of hard glittering tone and slackening that unrelenting intellectual tension which are necessary conditions of its characteristic effect; and he therefore rightly left them out. Equally is it silly to blame Milton for describing the garden of Eden in *Paradise Lost* without that vivid particularity of detail that is so delightful in *L'Allegro*. The effect of sublime grandeur he aimed at and the classical, generalized style by which he sought to convey it, alike excluded such detail. Form conditions matter as much as the artist's personality does. The reader must learn not to quarrel with this conditioning.

All this should put us on our guard against starting to read any book with a preconceived idea of what it ought or ought not to be like. For this reason rigid systems of aesthetic law—rules of design and composition and vocabulary, and so on—are to be viewed with suspicion. No doubt all good works of art have certain common characteristics, like unity, pattern, style. But these can be achieved in many different ways. For, since each work is the record of a new vision, it must to a certain extent evolve its own new form and explore its own new subject-matter. The so-called laws of art are only tentative generalizations drawn from the observation of particular works; and cannot completely apply to any original work. The eighteenth-century French critics who condemned Shakespeare for not observing the three unities are justly thought foolish: equally foolish is the modern reviewer who rebukes a poet for not employing what he hideously calls a 'contemporary vocabulary'. The only test of a book's merit is the impression it makes on the reader. If the reader is pleased, it does not matter how many so-called rules of art the author has broken.

The fact that any genuine work of art is unique should also discourage us from the seductive practice of ranking writers; drawing up a neat class list of the mighty dead, with firsts, seconds, and thirds judiciously awarded—Milton a safe first, Gray a safe second, Wordsworth just a first, in spite of some shockingly bad papers, etc. You can treat examination candidates in this way, for they are all engaged in doing the same papers and answering the same questions. But each creative writer is, as it were, doing a different paper which he has set himself. To treat them all as if they were the same and to mark them all accordingly is to misunderstand the nature of their activity. Our object should be rather, first to discover what questions the writer has asked himself; and then, in the light of that knowledge, to discover how far he is successful. No doubt, some writers are greater than others. Milton is a greater poet than Herrick because his creative imagination embraced a far wider and more important area of human experience in the field of its operation. But he is not a better poet in the sense that he succeeds more perfectly in his object. *Gather ye rosebuds while ye may* would not have been improved if Herrick had tried to make it more like *Lycidas*. It would have been totally different. When we come to considering writers of more comparable powers, ranking appears even more futile and irrelevant. Who shall say with any certainty whether Gray's *Elegy written in a Country Churchyard* ranks above or below Shelley's *Ode to the West Wind*? Each is a sincere and profoundly felt comment on matter of equally serious moment to mankind; each is executed with a supreme accomplishment. Which one happens to prefer depends surely on the bias of personal temperament. Anyway, Milton and Herrick, Gray and Shelley are, as artists, all much more like each other than any of them is like a bad writer. Critics love dividing literature up into categories, distinguishing between major art and minor art, primitive art and decadent art, light art and serious art, healthy art and morbid art. There is no harm in their doing this—it can even be illuminating—as long as they remember that the only really important distinction is that between good and bad art. To a just taste there is more in common between Tennyson and T. S. Eliot than between either of them and Martin Tupper. For the same reason, it is a mistake to range schools or periods of literature in order of merit, though no doubt some have been more prolific of masterpieces than others. On the whole, however, the difference between them is between mode of expression rather than height of achievement. In itself, Elizabethan tragedy is not a better or a worse form than French classical tragedy; it is another sort of form. As Pater said:

The critic will always remember that beauty exists in many forms. To him all periods, types, schools of taste, are in themselves equal. In all ages there have been some excellent workmen and some excellent work done. The question he asks is always: 'In whom did the stir, the genius, the sentiment of the period find itself? Where was the receptacle of its refinement, its elevation, its taste?' 'The ages are all equal,' said William Blake, 'but genius is always above its age.'

Genius—the distinguishing quality of the individual genius, that is what matters. There are as many different kinds of good book as there are different kinds of good writer. Each has something to give us. We should admire each in so far as he strikes us as good in his particular kind.

This further entails taking care to see that we are looking at a work from a point of view from which its aesthetic qualities occupy our centre of vision. We do this naturally with a piece of music, for music is a pure art and makes no appeal other than an aesthetic one. But literature, as we have seen, is not a pure art. Books can be regarded as social documents, as moral lessons, or as pieces of biography, and grouped together accordingly; often with confusing results for the reader who is seeking to estimate them as works of art. Thomas Hardy, for instance, like the realistic novelists who were his contemporaries, was a rebel against the old-fashioned orthodox ideas of his age about sex and religion. In consequence he has often been taken to be the same kind of author; and as such has been rightly judged a failure. The man who opens

Jude the Obscure expecting a sober, documented study of nineteenth-century working-class life, like *Esther Waters*, will naturally be disappointed. But, aesthetically, Hardy was a very old-fashioned writer. His conception of a good novel, formalized, romantic, and sensational, was much more like Sir Walter Scott's than it was like that of the young George Moore. It is only when we realize this and adjust our angle of vision accordingly—looking for similar qualities and making similar allowances, as we should when reading the Waverley novels—that Hardy's genius reveals itself in its full magnificence. Again I have noticed that some admirers of Pope do not like Tennyson. And it is true that the moral and intellectual opinions of these two authors are very different. That characteristic Victorian blend of doubt and aspiration, high-mindedness and muddle-headedness, which Tennyson voiced so melodiously, is at the very opposite pole from Pope's elegant, Augustan rationality. This intellectual difference, however, does not alter the fact that, aesthetically, Pope and Tennyson are akin. Neither was an original thinker—that is why each reflects so exactly the mind of his period—and both were possessed of a delicate sensibility to the beautiful and an extraordinary natural talent for writing, which they deliberately cultivated to the highest pitch of exquisite virtuosity. They should appeal to the same taste in art. But to realize this the reader must be looking, first of all, for artistic satisfaction. A writer can easily belong to one school intellectually and morally, and to another aesthetically. It is towards his aesthetic character that our eyes should be directed.

So much for the right approach; but our apprenticeship in literary appreciation is not over when we have achieved the right approach. We must also learn to understand the language in which the work is presented. Not just language in the literal sense but language as a metaphor for the whole mode in which the artist expresses himself. This means first of all the language of form, the convention he uses. Failure to understand this has led critics otherwise distinguished and discriminating to say very silly things. Matthew Arnold, for example, calls Pope 'a classic of prose', because he has never adjusted his mind to accept the rigid formality of the Augustan couplet as a vehicle for that serious passion and imaginative sensibility which he rightly thought essential qualities of great poetry. Again, the pundits of nineteenth-century conservative dramatic criticism refused to recognize Ibsen as a tragic dramatist because, unlike Shakespeare, he wrote about contemporary middle-class life and made his characters speak in modern colloquial language. At the very same time William Archer, who did know how to appreciate Ibsen, was denying any merit to Webster, because his plots were, from the realist's point of view, fantastic and incoherent. Inability to grasp a convention different from that to which they were accustomed prevented both from recognizing that in their different modes Ibsen and Webster were great dramatists of essentially the same type, masters of high and sombre tragedy. Strenuous critics of the psychological and sociological schools often pour scorn on scholars for devoting their time to elucidating the conventions, formal and linguistic, of past ages, instead of occupying themselves in the glorious task of exploring the economic background of authors, or analysing their repressions. But without the work of the scholars, it is impossible to get near the authors at all. It is they who teach us the language through which their economic and psychological situations are expressed.

So also do <u>historians</u>. In addition to the <u>language</u> of the form we must learn the language of the age. Past periods are like foreign countries; regions inhabited by men of like passions to our own, but with different customs and codes of behaviour. If we do not know these we shall misunderstand their actions and misapprehend their motives. It is the same with the natives of past ages. Poor Jane Austen is sometimes solemnly rebuked for snobbishness; and it is true that she has none of our curious modern prudery about mentioning social distinctions which everybody knows to exist, and which, in fact, most people set great store by. But this is because she lived in an age when social distinctions were taken for granted as a right and necessary feature of society. As a matter of fact, she is the opposite of snobbish in the true meaning of the word. She thinks it ridiculous of Lady Catherine de Bourgh to object to her nephew marrying the enchanting Elizabeth Bennet because she comes from a vulgar family. Unless we know something of the world she lived in, however, we may judge her as we might be tempted to judge a contemporary who referred to social distinctions with her blithe frankness. Some knowledge of history is, I am afraid, an essential preliminary to appreciation.

Finally, we have to learn to understand and accept the language of the author's temperament—to school ourselves to look at the world from his point of view while we are reading his books. This is much the hardest part of our training; for our own personal feelings are so much involved in it. Have we not temperaments of our own which may well be different to his and possibly anti-pathetic? Are we to treat these disrespect-fully? Pride, the sin of Lucifer and literary critics, rises in outraged protest against so humiliating a proposal. Sometimes it is our natural taste in manner or style which rebels. A reader with a temperamental preference for the sober and restrained will find it hard to persuade himself into a mood to appreciate the grotesque extravagance of phrase with which Browning so admirably expresses his natural idiosyncrasy. Someone who instinc-tively responds to the bold splendour of Hopkins' verbal invention may scarcely notice, let alone enjoy, the subtle and un-obtrusive felicity with which Bridges uses the English language. Or our antipathy may be moral. The puritan will recoil instinctively from Sterne, the pacifist from Kipling, the man of faith from Gibbon, the infidel from

Bunyan. Yet Hopkins and Bridges, Bunyan and Gibbon, Kipling and Sterne, are all in their different manners and degrees genuine artists. He who aspires to be a man of taste should suffer from a sense of failure if he does not enjoy them all. To do so, however, may mean subjecting himself to a stern course of self-discipline and self-effacement: he may have to learn to subdue his tenderly cherished prejudices, silence his garrulous self-important opinions if he is to attain to that receptive state of mind in which he can freely and spontaneously surrender himself to the book which he has chosen to study. Some people never even try to do these things, though they devote their lives to literary criticism. They take their first raw instinctive reactions as axiomatic: and instead of striving to widen their sympathies and correct their taste, spend their energies in constructing a philosophy of aesthetics to justify these first reactions. So stupendous a genius as Tolstoy lapsed in this way. He read *King Lear* and did not like it: his taste was for something more

THE FINE ART OF READING

realistic and restrained. It did not, however, strike him that he was suffering from a defect of sensibility in failing to respond to what had pleased generations of cultivated and intelligent persons. On the contrary, he at once made up his mind, not only that *King Lear* was no good, but that its admirers enjoyed it in reality as little as he did; and he wasted much of his valuable time and intellect in evolving a theory as to how and why they deceived themselves so strangely. Such are the deplorable results of not learning the language of an author's temperament before sitting in judgment on him.

Of course, human beings are of their nature imperfect: and our temperamental inclination will, whatever we do, always impair in some degree our capacity for appreciation. Myself, I fear I shall never enjoy George Meredith's novels as much as they deserve. It is not just that Meredith's faults jar on me; twenty years' conscientious, if intermittent, effort have proved me unable to view his works in a focus in which the beauty and intellectual penetration, whose presence I do genuinely perceive, is not somehow fogged and distorted by my temperamental distaste for his particular brand of stylistic floridity. On the other hand, Jane Austen's art and views are both so peculiarly sympathetic to me that it is possible, though I think improbable, that I overrate her. But the fact that a man can never hope to be perfectly virtuous is no reason for him not to try to be as virtuous as he can. Nor should the consciousness that we shall never completely attain our ideal stop us from striving as far as possible to achieve a perfectly just and catholic taste.

In fact, we can broaden our aesthetic sympathies far more than we expect to, when we start to try. The taste grows supple and flexible by training. And though the pleasure we attain by effort is never quite so rich as that which comes to us immediately, it is a peculiarly pure and disinterested one—and touched with a special zest from the trouble which it has cost us. The spirit experiences an extraordinary sense of expansion and exaltation when, after a long and arduous process of self-adjustment, it suddenly finds itself responding for the first time spontaneously and delightedly to a hitherto-unappreciated author.

Nor does our taste grow undiscriminating as it grows catholic. Greater breadth of sympathy makes us more detached, less partisan, readier to recognize that even our favourites are fallible. The more we are alive to remark the presence of the aesthetic quality, the more certainly do we perceive its absence. How few authors, we note, perfectly fulfil either their personal or their formal impulses! Some stray outside their creative range, choose to write about experience which does not stimulate their imaginations; as Scott does when he leaves that Scottish life which he understood so intimately, in order to try recreating the world of the English Middle Ages which he did not know at all, and so can only embody in the figures of conventional puppets, elaborately described suits of armour with no flesh and blood human beings inside them. Or the vision itself may be confused by inconsistency. Thackeray urges us to admire Lady Castlewood for her noble character at the same moment that he is vividly representing her as selfish, petty, and jealous: Byron proclaims his indifference to public opinion with a loudness of tone that only betrays his secret anxiety that everybody should be impressed by him. In the works of both the trained taste is quick to detect a false note.

It also becomes skilled to notice when an author's formal impulse does not find satisfactory fulfilment; to remark, for example, that many minor Elizabethan dramatists come to grief for want of some central principle of composition with which to integrate the varying elements of their play into a unity. The sub-plot has no organic relation to the main plot: the comic characters are drawn in a realistic convention, the serious in a wildly poetic one, so that it is impossible to believe in a world in which they are represented as existing side by side. Then there are the authors who do not recognize the nature

of their inspiration; and in consequence try to
express it in a radically unsuitable form.
Hardy does this in *Two on a Tower*, where he
takes a theme appropriate to a concentrated
and lyrical verse tale, and then attempts, by
filling it up with a clutter of conventional
intrigue, to swell it out to the length required
for a Victorian three-volume novel. Other
authors' again fail to perceive the limitations
of their medium. This is the chief cause of
Wordsworth's notorious inequality. He did
not realize that to put a statement into verse
form gives it emphasis, and that therefore it
must be a statement that will bear emphasiz-
ing. As a result there is sometimes a comical
incongruity between the prosaic flatness of
what he says and the lilting song rhythm in
which he says it:

> For still the more he works, the more
> Do his weak ankles swell.

Scott, Hardy, Wordsworth—these are all
writers of the highest quality of genius. To be

able to appreciate them is almost the test of a fine taste. But our capacity to do so will not make us notice their lapses less. On the contrary, the habit of disengaging the aesthetic element makes us the more acutely aware of the mass of lifeless and unaesthetic matter, in which it is all too often embedded.

However, the gain is immensely greater than the loss. To train our taste is to increase our capacity for pleasure: for it enables us to enter into such a variety of experience. This indeed is the special precious power of literature. In actual life our experience is inevitably restricted both by the limitations imposed by circumstances and by our own character. No one person can ever know in practice what it is like to be both a man and a woman, a mystic and a materialist, a criminal and a pillar of society, an ancient Roman and a modern Russian. But books can teach us to be all these things in imagination. Every reader is a Lady of Shalott, who, secluded in his secret chamber, forgets the hours, as he sits watching the endless procession of human thought and passion and action, as it passes, motley and tumultuous, across the gleaming mirror of literature.

And, like the Lady of Shalott's, it is a magic mirror. For all that it reflects is transmuted by the alchemy of art into matter for delight. This is very odd, considering how little delightful experience often is; how dull or trivial or painful, or unedifying! So also is the experience which forms the material of much great literature. In actual life it would be boring to live at Middlemarch, shocking to behave like the characters in *Love for Love*, depressing to look at mankind as Gulliver learnt to do, horrifying to find the story of *King Lear* occurring among one's acquaintance. Yet one enjoys them all in literature. Indeed the worst is the most enjoyable. *King Lear* provides the most satisfying experience of the lot. How can this be? It is no answer to say—as is sometimes said—that what we enjoy is not the subject, but the skill with which it is presented. Literary skill means ability to present a subject as accurately and vividly as possible. A distressing story, vividly and accurately presented, should therefore strike us as particularly distressing. Further, even were it true that a skilful presentation of a painful story did give pleasure by its skill, an agreeable story presented with equal skill should be even more delightful. But this is not so. *Twelfth Night* is not a more satisfying work than *King Lear*. We should not like *King Lear* itself better if Cordelia was saved and all ended happily. Rather should we feel such an alteration to be an anticlimax. The ruthless determination with which Shakespeare pursues his theme to its appalling close contributes essentially to the feeling of sublime exaltation with which the tragedy inspires us. In the same way, to descend to less elevated spheres of achievement, we do not feel that *Gulliver's Travels* would be improved if Swift liked human beings better, or *Love for Love* if the characters in it took their marriage vows more seriously, or *Middlemarch* if a group of elegant and entertaining persons had chosen to set up house there. A work of art is certainly not delightful in proportion as it mirrors a delightful phase of experience.

This is a dark and paradoxical mystery, in whose shadow lurks the whole question of the fundamental significance of art. It is not for me to propose a final answer to a riddle from which some of the wisest of mankind have recoiled baffled. Apart from anything else, any such answer must inevitably differ according as people differ in their interpretation of the significance of human life as a whole; and so can never satisfy everyone. But since the ultimate purpose and value of that art of appreciation which is my subject is involved in the issue, I feel impelled to offer you a few tentative and incomplete thoughts on the matter. Why then should we feel that the experience given us by accomplished works of art, whatever their subject-matter, is agreeable; and not only agreeable, but also precious and illuminating? Surely the answer is to be found in the fact that the soul is born instinctively desiring order, harmony, beauty:

but finds itself in a world disorderly, dissonant, and in great part ugly. In consequence it is for ever unsatisfied. The very best of our experience is not as good as our dreams: our most exquisite moments are flawed and fragmentary. And they are ephemeral. Even as we gaze the sunset fades, the apple-blossom sheds itself and scatters. It is the peculiar virtue of art to present us with an image of perfection incarnate, to show us some aspect of earthly experience, circumstantial, concrete, and recognizable, yet mysteriously free from the imperfections which mar it in the real world. (The fleeting is apparently arrested in mid-flight.) 'Forever wilt thou love, and she be fair,' cries Keats ecstatically as he looks at the figures of the lovers graven on the Grecian Urn. And even the ugly elements in life are made by the artist a means of beauty. Grief and horror, drabness and deformity these are, as often as not, necessary strands in the web of enchantment which he weaves to take us captive. So that, when contemplating a work of art, our desire for perfection and

40

our sense of reality are reconciled. We feel ourselves relieved, if only for a moment, from the wearisome burden of our daily dissatisfaction. For once we accept an experience unreservedly: and with joy. Further, our joy is deeper in proportion as we are induced to accept what we normally find unacceptable, in proportion as the vision, presented to us by the artist, includes aspects of life which in our everyday existence, distress us. For then his achievement represents a more signal and extraordinary victory over the ills of our mortal condition. There is a greater spiritual triumph in accepting Cordelia's sufferings than in accepting Viola's happiness. Thus tragedy brings glory out of the very stuff of despair; in it we are made to face life at its most baffling and dreadful, and yet to see it as a thing of beauty and a joy for ever.

Nor is this impression false; an opium vision conjured up to dull and disguise the brutality of fact. If it were, it would not be so deeply strengthening to the soul. No—life is revealed to us more clearly when we see it reflected in the Lady of Shalott's mirror: Shakespeare's view of reality is truer than our own, as well as more beautiful. For the perfection, of which he gives us a glimpse, is no delusive daydream. Serene and changeless, it exists with a far more intense reality than the transitory world that we see around us, and which is, at its best, but its blurred and flickering shadow. Listen to Sir Thomas Browne:

Whosoever is harmonically composed, delights in harmony; which makes me much distrust the symmetry of those heads which declaim against all Church-Musick. For myself, not only from my obedience, but my particular Genius, I do embrace it: for even that vulgar and Tavern-Musick, which makes one man merry and another mad, strikes in me a deep fit of devotion, and a profound contemplation of the first Composer. There is something in it of Divinity more than the ear discovers: it is an Hieroglyphical and shadowed lesson of the whole World, and creatures of God;

such a melody to the ear, as the whole World well understood, would afford the understanding. In brief, it is a sensible fit of that harmony, which intellectually sounds in the ears of God.

For me, this is the most illuminating statement ever made about art. In it, as by a flash of unearthly divination, Browne reveals art's function in the scheme of creation, and also the mode in which it is performed. The artist, he suggests, converts the imperfect into an image of perfection, not by softening or omitting ugly facts—if he did, he would shake our confidence in his work as a true picture of the reality we know—but rather by presenting these ugly facts as the component parts of a perfect order and harmony. Further, the passage illustrates how any work of art does this, whatever its substance. Not some celestial strain of Byrd or Orlando Gibbons is it, but 'vulgar and tavern-musick' that strikes in Browne his deep fit of devotion. So also with literature. Any phase of human feeling, however trifling, any point of view, however dismal or perverse, can be transmuted into an image of spiritual perfection—slighter no doubt than that evoked for us by Dante, yet an image of spiritual perfection all the same. The author may not have intended it to be. But he cannot help himself. By a sublime irony, not only pious Herbert and mystical Blake, but mocking Byron and irresponsible Sterne and worldly Congreve and despairing Hardy, are, in Sir Thomas Browne's sense of the word, devotional authors. For in so far as they have expressed their spirit in the harmony of a true work of art, they have opened the eyes of the soul to a sight of that divine and flawless essence whence it springs and for which, while its unquiet exile on earth endures, it is immedicably homesick.